Enterprise and history

CHARLES WILSON

[Photograph by Barry Supple]

Enterprise and history

Essays in honour of Charles Wilson

Edited by

D. C. COLEMAN

and

PETER MATHIAS

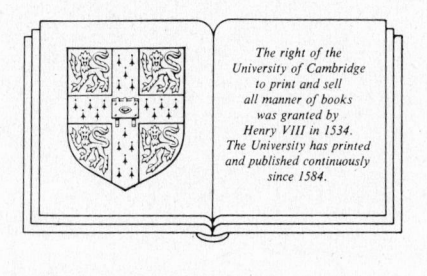

The right of the
University of Cambridge
to print and sell
all manner of books
was granted by
Henry VIII in 1534.
The University has printed
and published continuously
since 1584.

CAMBRIDGE UNIVERSITY PRESS

Cambridge
London   New York   New Rochelle
Melbourne   Sydney

Published by the Press Syndicate of the University of Cambridge
The Pitt Building, Trumpington Street, Cambridge CB2 1RP
32 East 57th Street, New York, NY 10022, USA
296 Beaconsfield Parade, Middle Park, Melbourne 3206, Australia

© Cambridge University Press 1984

First published 1984

Printed in Great Britain at the University Press, Cambridge

Library of Congress catalogue card number: 83-26329

British Library Cataloguing in Publication Data

Enterprise and History.
I. Business – History
II. Coleman, D.C.C. II. Mathias, Peter
III. Wilson, Charles, *1914–*
338.6′09 HF5341

ISBN 0 521 24951 1

TM

Contents

v

Contents